To:

From:

FRIENDS

Knock Your Socks Off!

By Dee Lindner

 PETER PAUPER PRESS, INC.
White Plains, New York

*For my best friends
Gary, Puddy, and Snuffy*

Designed by Heather Zschock

Copyright © 2008 Sock Monkey Lady, Inc.
Published by Peter Pauper Press, Inc.
202 Mamaroneck Avenue
White Plains, New York 10601
ISBN 978-1-59359-898-3

Printed in China

7   6   5   4

Visit us at www.peterpauper.com

FRIENDS

Knock Your Socks Off!

Introduction

In this tribute to true friends, red-heel sock monkeys teach us everything we need to know about friendship. Like friends, sock monkeys help us gain a foothold on life whenever we feel out of shape. As sole-mates, they know how to spin a yarn, and they help us not to take things too seriously by monkeying around. Whenever we are frayed, they remind us to take life one stitch at a time and not to pop a seam. They keep us on our toes and help us to mend our ways. They are there when we

Friends
come in all
different
shapes
sizes.

are head over heels in love and when we are hung out to dry. In other words, sock monkeys—like friends—keep us from coming unraveled.

Friendship isn't just about comfort, though; it's ab inspiration, about feelir as we discover that certain monkey there for each down, and come our can't he

Friends keep your secrets safe.

Friends create lasting memories.

Friends
are all
heart.

Friends play around.

Friends lend a helping hand.

Friends go the distance.

Friends lift your spirits.

Friends calm rough waters.

Friends love to stir up fun.

Friends
heal
wounded
hearts.

Friends giggle snort!

Friends keep you on your toes.

Friends spell **LOVE** *in all different ways.*

Friends encourage dreams and desires.

Friends harvest good times.

Friends are full of trick-or-treats.

Friends are a work of art.

Friends are a great gift.

Friends rock!

Friends drive each other bananas!

Friends are good-natured.

Friends don't tell tales.

Friends chill out together.

Friends
hang out
together.

Friends pile on the fun.

Friends suit each other.

Friends overlook your faults.

Friends are the cat's meow.

Friends are there in rain or shine.

Friends give you hugs and kisses.

Friends listen closely.

Friends are priceless treasures.

Friends
double
the fun.

Friends make everything all right.

Friends give you an edge.

Friends rise to the occasion.

Friends cheer the smallest success.

Friends are picture-perfect.

Friends let it all hang out.

Friends stay connected.